Total T[illegible] with

Discover th[illegible] Improve Your Productivity with Evernote in 2 Hours

Dominic Wolff

ORGANIZED LIVING
PRESS

Atlanta, Georgia USA

ISBN 978-14953-632-8-3

9 781495 363283 >

Dominic Wolff

What Our Readers Are Saying

"I found this guide very useful as it taught me all I needed to know about Evernote, the most practical of tools."

★★★★☆ Steven Torres, Charleston

"I've started using Evernote only recently with good results, but it wasn't until I've read this book that I've realized its full potential. Essential reading for all the users."

★★★★☆ John Durbin, Iowa

"Evernote is a great tool, but if you don't know how to use it, things can become a little complicated. To avoid wasting your precious time read this guide. It will make your life easier."

★★★★☆ Essie Lander, Ohio

Foreword

There are a lot of reasons why someone should use Evernote, and there is at least one good reason that somebody should buy this guide: it is really useful to those that really want know how to make the best out of this particular software.

Evernote was designed to help people get things done. As we live in a world where speed is everything, we need to keep up with the times, but in order to accomplish that we have to be organized. Evernote is a useful tool that can take us a step forward in that direction; but every tool needs a good manual, and this volume aspires to be exactly that.

In these pages you'll find the answers to any questions you may have, tips and advice on how to use the program, detailed explanations about the different ways it can be of service and much more. It doesn't matter if you are a professional or not; one way or another Evernote can help make your life much easier.

So, forget all you know about how things used to work and welcome to the new era; an era of change and technological advances, and an era where the solutions to most of your problems lie just a click, and a guide away.

Thank you for downloading my book. Please REVIEW this book. I need your feedback to make the next version better. Thank you so much!

TABLE OF CONTENTS

DISCLAIMER

While all attempts have been made to provide effective, verifiable information in this Book neither the Author nor Publisher assumes any responsibility for errors, inaccuracies, or omissions. Any slights of people or organizations are unintentional.

Introduction

Whether you're a student, a professional, a stay-at-home parent, a freelancer, an executive, an academic, or between jobs, you need to stay organized. Everyone has a lot of information, tasks, and ideas that they have floating around in their heads (and often on a lot of Post-its as well), and after a while, you may start to forget things. Evernote exists so you have a place to store all of that information so you can keep track of it, organize it, and retrieve it at any time.

Evernote is a free application that you can download to your computer, phone, or tablet so that no matter where you are, you have access to all of your notes—you can read what you've written, look at things you scanned, edit old notes, and write new ones. You can even take pictures on your phone and import them directly into Evernote so you can have a record of them. No matter what you want to remember, group, tag, or sort, and whether you have a Windows computer, a Mac, an iPhone, an Android phone, a Blackberry, a Samsung Galaxy Note, or an iPad, you can keep it all organized from a single app.

And with the tips, tricks, and tutorials in this book, you'll be an Evernote expert in no time. We'll start with the basics—signing up for an account, downloading the application to your computer and your phone, and getting your first notebook set up. I'll share some advanced tips, like using tags and reminders, and we'll also delve into some really useful things: how to use Evernote at home and at work to streamline your life. Let's get started!

A (very) brief overview of Evernote

If you've never heard of Evernote, you might be wondering what sort of complicated, high-tech software I'm talking about that can help you so much in getting your life organized. You might be surprised to find out that it's actually quite simple in design—when you strip away all of the extra features, Evernote is just a note-taking app. It allows you to create notes, sort them into notebooks, add tags (labels), and sort those notebooks into stacks. Of course, a lot of those extra features are the ones that make Evernote such a great app—and these are the things that we'll be discussing in this book.

How Evernote will change your life

This seems like a lot of hype for a note-taking app, doesn't it? After all, no one has ever said that Apple's Notes app will change your life. However, Evernote provides the capability to very easily sort, categorize, and retrieve information. You can keep a huge amount of information in Evernote and find it very quickly, even if it's buried deep within one of your notebooks. Evernote works very well as an information repository, thus it can take the form of something like a personal encyclopedia—all the information and random ideas you find interesting or useful can be stored here. You can store useful things for your professional life and career, things at home, useful information for your family, and anything else you can think of. There's no limit to what Evernote can help you organize.

Where this, especially comes in handy is when you're trying to increase your productivity. The Getting Things Done (GTD) personal management system is perfect for Evernote. The idea at the core of this system is that if you get absolutely everything in your head down on paper, you'll never be able to forget any of it, and you can set up reminders and checks that will enable you to stay on top of all of your tasks. Although this book isn't about GTD, I'll mention it a few times, and I encourage you to check it out, either online or in another book that I've written, "Master Getting Things Done the David Allen Way with Evernote." Evernote and GTD weren't designed with each other in mind, but a lot of people have come to associate them with each other, as they're an almost-perfect match.

Getting Started with Evernote

In this section, I'll walk you through all of the steps to get Evernote up and running, and answer a few questions along the way. If you're already somewhat familiar with Evernote, you should still read this section, as there's always a chance that you'll learn something new!

Installing Evernote

Because Evernote is so popular, you might already have on the app in one of your devices (whether you downloaded it or it came pre-installed). If you do, you can skip this section, though I do recommend downloading Evernote on all of your devices, which is likely your computer and your phone. Fortunately, installing Evernote on any system is pretty simple. I'd recommend downloading Evernote on your laptop or desktop computer before getting on your mobile devices, as creating an account is easier with a full-size keyboard.

Installing Evernote on a Mac

Go to www.evernote.comwww.evernote.com/evernote and click on the highlighted download button. The download should start immediately. Once the download has completed, click on the disk image that's now in your Downloads folder to open it. Drag the Evernote icon to the Applications folder icon, and you're done!

Installing Evernote on Windows

Just like with a Mac, start by going to www.evernote.com/evernote/ and clicking the download button. A download will start. Once it's done, open the .exe file that just downloaded and follow the instructions to install the program.

Creating an account

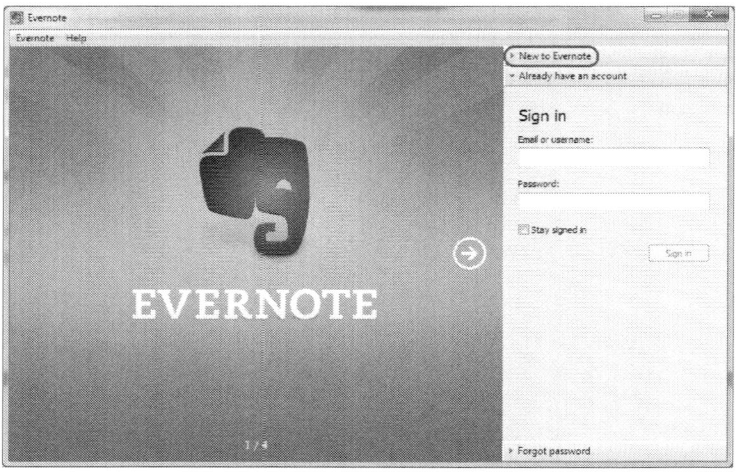

Open up the app on your computer (or your mobile device, if you so choose) and you'll be prompted for a username and a password. If this is your first time using Evernote, you'll need to create a new account. Just click the link to create a new account and follow the instructions. You'll need to choose a username and password and enter some information—name, e-mail address, and so on—and then you'll receive an e-mail to confirm your e-mail address. Once you've done that, you're all set to go.

During the account creation process, you'll be asked whether you want a free account or a premium one. For now, select a free one. In the next section, I'll go over the differences between the two, and you can decide for yourself which is best for you.

Installing Evernote on iOS

If you've ever downloaded an app for iOS, you already know how to get Evernote. Simply pull up the App Store and search for "Evernote." It should come up right away—click "Install" and it'll start downloading. Once it's downloaded, open it up and enter the password that you chose on your desktop (you'll use the same username and password on all of your devices).

Installing Evernote on Android

Android is just as simple as iOS. Open the Google Play Store and search for the Evernote app in their database. Hit "Install" to download it, and once it's been downloaded, sign in.

Installing Evernote on Windows 8

Go to the Windows Store (either on your desktop computer or mobile device) and search for "Evernote." You'll need to click or touch the "Install" button to install the app on your device.

Other operating systems

Evernote can also be installed on other operating systems, like WebOS (found on PalmPre and Pixi devices), BlackBerry OS, and Windows Mobile (on the Windows Phone). Just go to wherever you would normally download an app and search for "Evernote."

Free or Premium?

Once you start using Evernote on a regular basis, you'll probably realize just how powerful it is and—if you're like me—you'll be more than happy to pay $5 per month (or $45 per year) for some of the extra features and to support the company.

If you're an educational user, you can get a 50% discount on the premium price. Just go to

http://evernote.com/about/premium/groups/education.ph/ to find out more.

Here's a breakdown of the features that you get with each membership.

Free accounts

1. Monthly uploads of up to 60 MB per month
2. Up to 25 MB total space for each note created
3. The ability to share notes with other Evernote users
4. Text and handwriting recognition
5. The ability to attach many types of files to your notes

Premium accounts

1. The ability to search attached PDFs
2. No ads
3. PIN lock for Android and iOS devices
4. Faster image search
5. Up to 100 MB of space per note
6. Search past versions of the notes
7. Share notes and allow other users to edit
8. Local storage of notes on iOS and Android devices
9. Priority tech support
10. Increased upload limit (1 GB per month)

I recommend that just about everyone upgrade to a premium account after using Evernote for a while, both for the added features and to help keep Evernote around (the company makes money through advertising, but a regular income stream from account holders is important, too). If you're going to be using Evernote for business, you might want to upgrade right away—being able to share notebooks and allow others to edit them, and the increased upload capacity is really valuable when you're working with a lot of notes. And if you're going to be using Evernote for a large business, the Business account option is worth looking into, as it provides even larger upload limits, increased storage space, and more collaborative options.

Your First Time Using Evernote

The goal of this book is to get you from total novice to expert in just a couple of hours. To get started on that, I'll first walk you through the layout of the Evernote window, and then you'll get some practice with using the app.

The Evernote Window

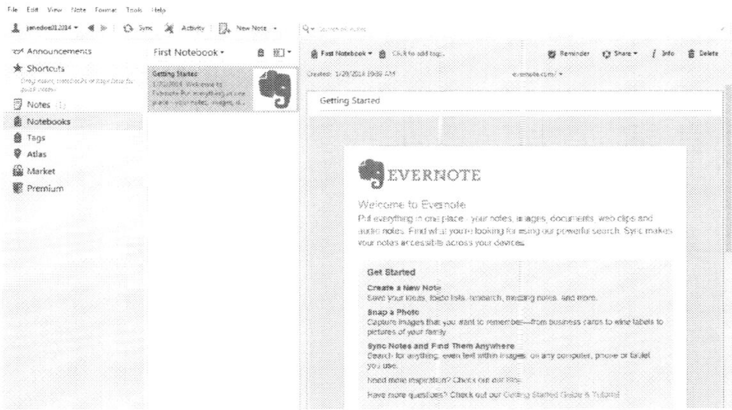

When you first open up Evernote, you won't see very much—just a notebook called "First Notebook," which will contain a single note called "Getting Started." Before playing around with the features, however, you should familiarize yourself with the layout of the Evernote window.

There are three main sections in the Evernote window:

1. The **sidebar**, where you'll navigate between different collections of your notes
2. The **note list**, where you can move between individual notes
3. The **note editor**, where you can create and edit notes

There are also toolbars at the top of the screen from which you can take a lot of common action. Let's take a look at each of these sections in greater detail.

Sidebar

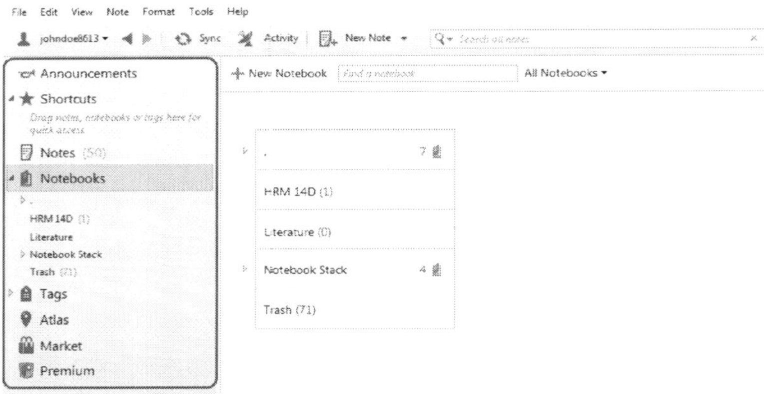

The sidebar allows you to view your notes in different groupings. For example, you can view all of the notes in your account (I find this to be very useful when I know that I created a note recently but can't remember where I put it); view the notes that are in a certain notebook and the name for a collection of notes; view all of the notes that are in the same stack (a grouping of notebooks), giving you a higher-level view of your notes; view your notes by tags, which we'll come to in a bit; and finally, you can view your notes by the location where they were created, and if you've tagged them with this information (personally, I rarely do this, as there doesn't seem to be much of a point, but it could be fun if you use Evernote around the world, I suppose).

Note list

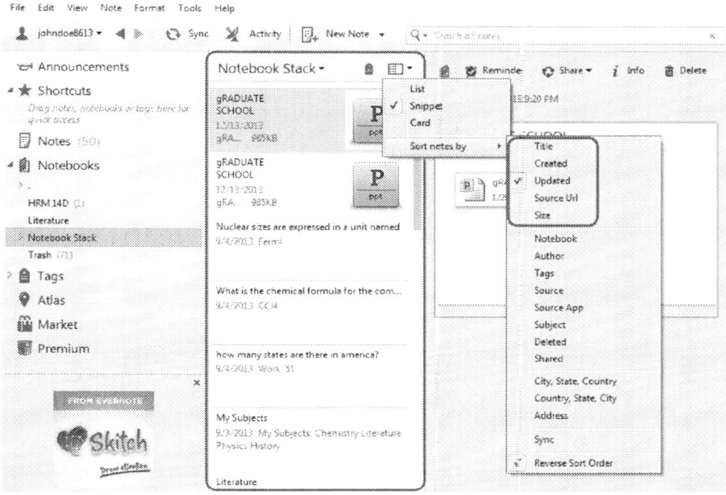

When you select a notebook, stack, or tag, every note in that group shows up here, in the middle of the window. There are five different views that are available in the note list: card view, expanded card view, snippet view, side list view, and top list view. Select each of these in turn from the View menu and see how they change the note list. I prefer the snippet view, as it keeps the notes well-organized and shows the first line or two of the note, so you can get an idea of what it's about if you didn't title it very well (which often happens to me when I'm making notes on the go). You can also sort your notes in a number of ways: title, date created, date update, source URL, and size. You can choose the sorting method from the View Options button in the top-right corner of the note list. You can choose whichever sorting option you prefer, but don't feel limited to just one—you can always switch between options and use whichever one is most convenient for your current project.

Note editor

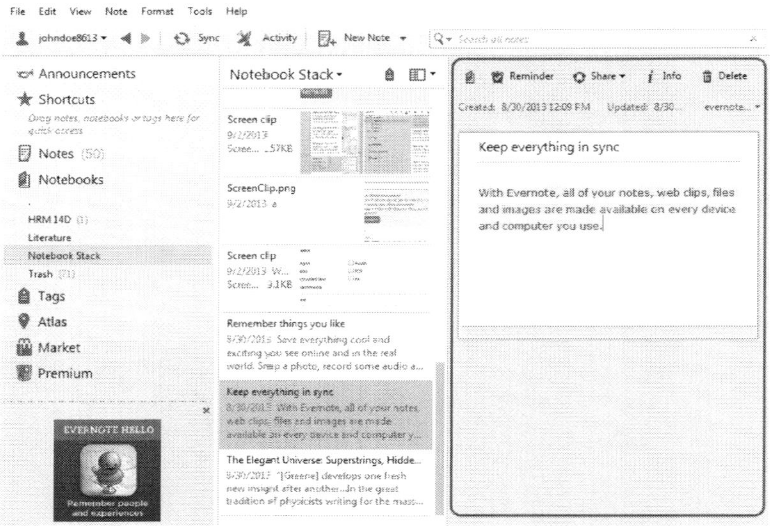

This is where you'll be doing most of the work in Evernote. When you click on a note in the list or create a new note, it'll appear in this window, where you can edit it. The note editor is very simple—just click where you want to type and start typing. The notes are always editable, and they save automatically (though it doesn't hurt to manually save them every once in a while). To add a tag to your note, just click on the tag bar and start typing. To change the notebook that your note is in, all you have to do is select the new notebook from the dropdown. You can make changes to formatting, add attachments, share the note via social networking sites, and setup reminders (more on these later), all from the note editor, making this the most important part of the Evernote window.

Evernote Basics

As I mentioned, when you first open Evernote you'll see one notebook with a single note in it. We'll be creating another notebook to practice some of the basic Evernote skills, but once we've gotten through this, you can rename, edit, or delete the automatically generated notebook.

The first step in GTD (and the first step you'll want to use with Evernote, no matter which personal management system you're using) is to process all of your "stuff" and classify them into a number of areas. You can choose what will work best for you, or experiment with different methods. For example, you could create areas for personal projects and work projects, and file more specific projects into those groups. In our example, we're going to use the project of writing a biography of Nikola Tesla and go through the steps of creating a new notebook, adding a note, and a few other things that will help you stay organized.

Step 1. Create a notebook.

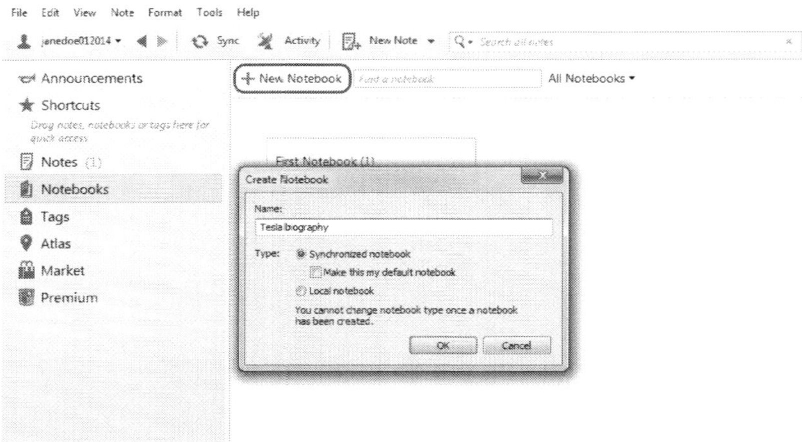

Let's create a notebook for your biography. There are a few ways to do this. You can click on the Notebooks tab in the sidebar and then press the "New Notebook" button at the top of the screen, or you can select "File" from the menu bar and click on "New Notebook." You can also use the key combination ctrl / command + shift + N. Evernote will ask you what you want to name the notebook—let's call it "Tesla biography." You'll also be given the choice of whether this will be a local or a synchronized notebook. A local notebook is available only on the computer used to create it, while a synchronized notebook is made available on any device associated with your account. I recommend using synchronized notebooks in almost all cases, so make this a synchronized one. Click "OK" and the notebook will appear with an open note pane.

Step 2. Create a note.

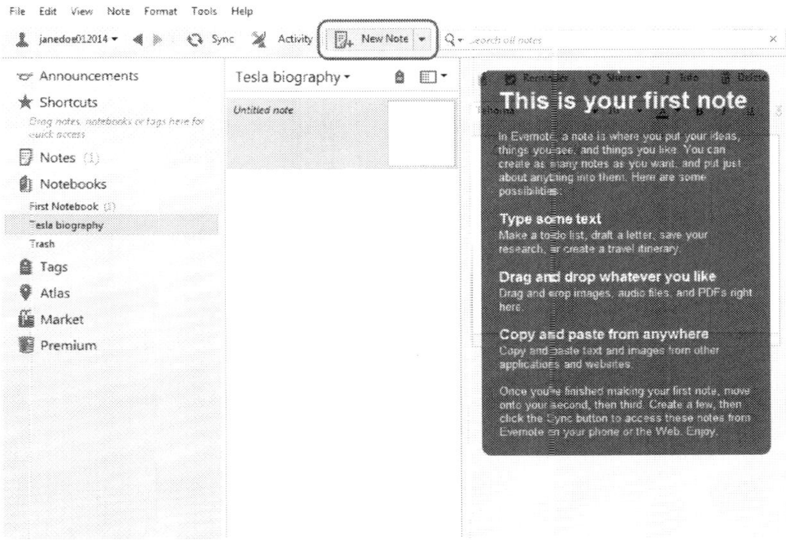

Open the Tesla biography notebook by either double clicking it on the note list or clicking it on the sidebar. Click on the "New Note" button at the top or press ctrl / command + N to create a new note. A new, untitled note is created instantly—using this keyboard command allows you to create new notes very quickly, which can be useful if you create a lot of notes in a day (which is very likely if you're going to be using GTD, especially at the beginning).

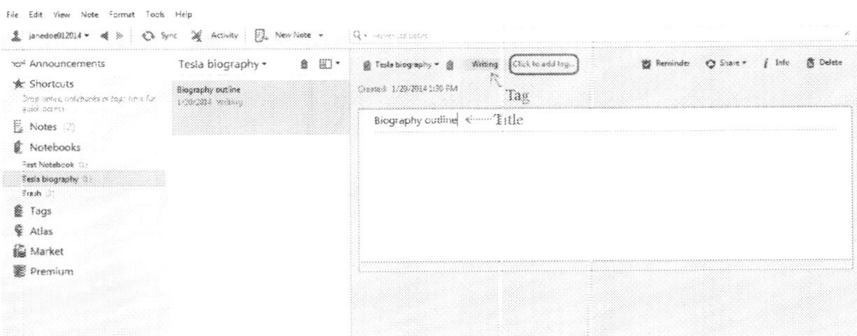

The cursor will automatically be in the title field, where it says "Untitled note"—type in a new title in the note editor, something like "Biography outline." You can also add tags now—click in the tags field and try it out. Add a few, like "Writing" and "Non-fiction." Eventually, you'll develop your own system of tags that will help you stay organized, but for now, just use these examples. When you have dozens of notebooks and hundreds of notes, specific tags will be very helpful.

If you're not sure how to start tagging your notes, you can use the following categories to get some ideas. Remember that you're not limited in the number of tags that you apply to a note, so use as many as you think will be useful. Here are a few pieces of information that you can use:

1. Person or place. The names of specific clients or even potential clients, make logical tags, and if your work or personal life revolves around certain places, those can be useful as well. For example, you might have "Home" and "Cabin" as tags.
2. General topic. Using our Tesla biography example, you could add tags like "Biography," "Writing," or "Tesla."
3. Specific topic. You can get more fine-grained here, too, and split up your notes with tags that include things like "Outline," "Introduction," "Research," and "Conclusion." If you're using Evernote for work, you could use terms like "Client pitch," "Saratoga project," and the like.
4. Source. If you're doing research of any sort, one of your tags could describe the source of your material. Did that note on

Nikola Tesla come from *Scientific American*? Make that a title a tag.

Step 3. Add your notebook to a stack.

Just like how notes are collected in notebooks, notebooks can be collected in stacks. You can have a stack for work, a stack for home, a stack for hobbies, and a stack related to things for your family. Or you could get more specific and have stacks for each project you're working on at work, each family member, each of your hobbies, and so on. I recommend erring on the side of having too many stacks—the more detailed your organizational system, the better!

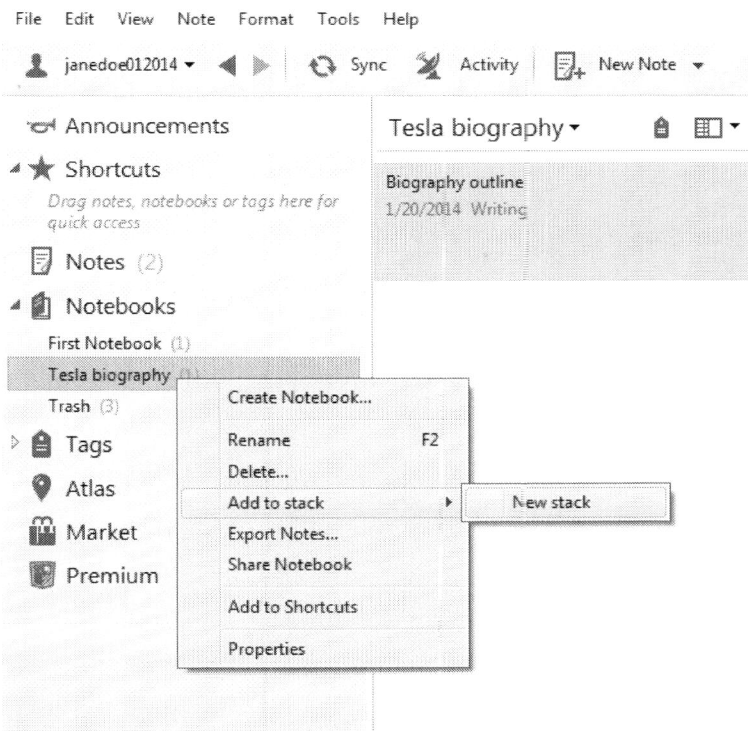

To add your Tesla biography notebook to a stack, go to the Notebooks tab in the sidebar and right-click on the notebook. Place your cursor over "Add to Stack," and select "New Stack." You should now see that your notebook is part of a stack called "Notebook Stack." Right-click on the stack and rename it "Writing."

This may not seem all that useful now, but once you have a lot of notebooks, you'll see the utility of stacks very quickly. My current stack of notebooks looks something like this:

- Academic
- Blogging
- Contracts
- Fashion
- Home
- Language learning
- Programming
- Recipes
- Technology
- Work projects

Each of those stacks has several notebooks. For example, my Blogging stack contains these notebooks:

- Content
- Marketing
- Monetization
- Pitch letters

- Planning
- SEO
- Social

By combining notebooks and stacks, you can create a great system of organization. You can think of your stacks and notebooks like the hierarchical folder structure on your computer, except that there are only three levels.

Now that you've created a note, a notebook, and a stack, you now have a good understanding of the basics of Evernote. While there's a lot more functionality available, you can probably get significantly more organized than you are right now just by using these steps and the search bar (in the top right corner of the screen). Now you're ready to move on and become a master of productivity with Evernote!

Become an Evernote Expert in Two Hours

If you're going to become an Evernote master, you're going to have to develop a few simple skills. I'll go over these skills here so you have an idea of what you should be doing, and then you can continue the learning on your own. First, though, a few prerequisites:

Prerequisites

1. Be able to create a note, notebook, and stack.

I went over these in the last section, but just in case you skipped to this chapter, make sure that you can create and rename these items. Take ten minutes to play around with the different menus, too—right-click on a notebook and move it to a different stack; rename a notebook; rename a note.

2. Download the web clipper.

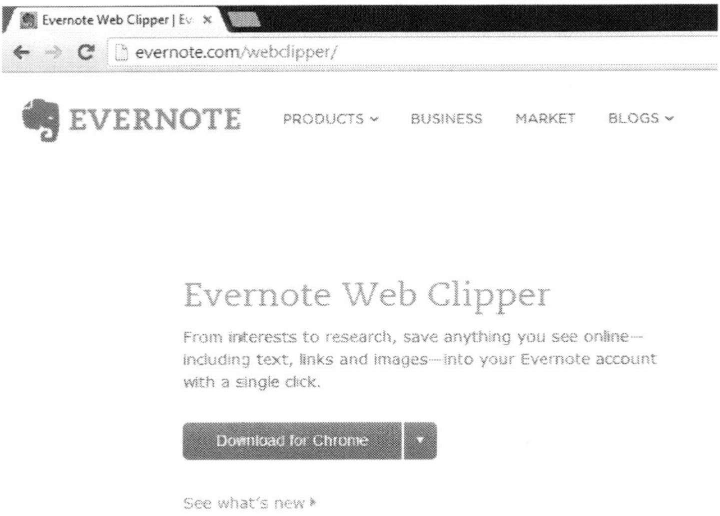

The web clipper is one of my favorite parts of Evernote, and something that will greatly aid you in your quest to become an organization guru. To download the web clipper, go to www.evernote.com/webclipper and follow the instructions. You can also get it through the Chrome Web Store. Make sure that it's installed in your browser.

3. Try a manual sync once or twice.

Evernote automatically syncs your desktop app with your online account, but sometimes you'll want to refresh it right away. Do this by clicking the sync button at the top of the screen, or by clicking File > Sync.

Capturing Information

To best make use of Evernote—especially with GTD—you're going to need to capture a lot of different kinds of information very efficiently and categorize that information into different notebooks or stacks. This section will give you an idea about some of the ways that you can use Evernote to store all sorts of information.

1. Drag and drop files into notes.

If you want to attach a file—like a Word document, an image, a spreadsheet, or an audio file—to a note, all you have to do is drag it from your file explorer (Windows Explorer for Windows, Finder for Mac) and drop it into an open note. Your note will now have an attachment.

This is great if you're keeping notes about a document in Evernote, or if you're going to use Evernote to move things through your workflow. In which case, you'll want to have your files immediately at hand.

2. Use the web clipper to record websites.

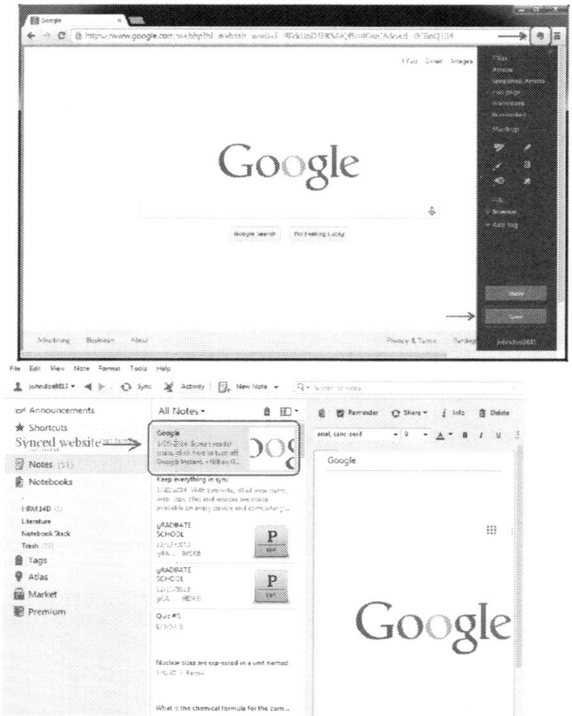

The web clipper is one of the most underutilized features of Evernote. By now, you should have it installed in your browser and you should be signed in (if you're not, go ahead and do that now by clicking on the icon in your toolbar). Now, all you have to do is navigate to a page that contains content you want to keep, and click on the web clipper in your browser toolbar. It'll present you with a few options for how much of the website it will keep, but for now, just select a notebook and hit "Save." Once you sync the Evernote app with your account, you'll see that a new note has been created with the content from that website already in it!

The big advantage of this over copying and pasting the URL is that you can access the page content while you're offline. And

Evernote keeps the URL for you, so you'll be able to go back to the page whenever you want. I use this all the time for recipes, driving directions, and images. One thing to get used to is selecting the right clipping option—for example, by using the "Article" option, Evernote will try to determine which part of the page is the most useful for you, which will save you a lot of space in the long run.

3. Create audio and video notes.

When you're on the go and you need to get something down really quickly, it might be most efficient to just create an audio or video note (especially when you only have your phone or tablet, which can slow down your typing). Click File > New Audio Note or File > New Webcam Note (or New Facetime Camera Note, if on a Mac), and hit the record button to start recording.

While you're likely to use this mostly for dictation-like purposes, there are actually quite a few different good uses of this function. You can record a class lecture, a workshop speaker, or any other sort of presentation; capture a quick video to share via Evernote; create a video diary; or even take a video of the damage to your car in case of an accident. The possibilities are endless once you get the hang of it! Just remember that notes have a 25 or 100MB size limit, depending on the type of your account, and audio and video notes can reach this size quickly.

4. Scan documents into notes.

Many scanners—like the Fujitsu ScanSnap Evernote Edition, the Brother ImageCenter ADS 1500W, and the Canon P-215—now come with the ability to interface with Evernote, so you can scan documents directly into notes, which is great for organizing receipts, expenses, taxes, leases, and other important documents. Even if your scanner doesn't have this ability, it's easy to drag and drop files into notes, as discussed a few paragraphs ago. Windows users also have the option to create an Evernote import folder (discussed below), which allows you to place files in the folder and have them automatically imported into Evernote. Just point your scanner at this folder, and your scanned documents will show up in Evernote.

Even if you don't have a scanner, you can use your smart phone or tablet camera to do much the same thing! The quality likely won't be as high, but it'll still allow you to keep organized records of your important documents.

5. Use Evernote's import folder to speed up file attachments.

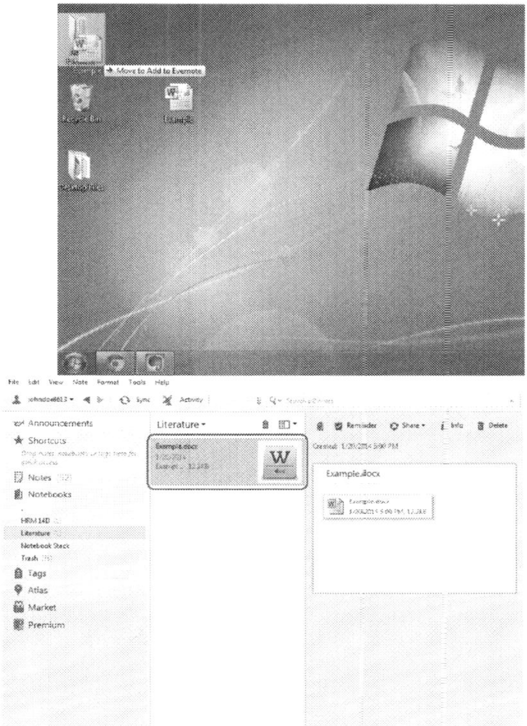

If you're using Evernote on a Windows computer, you have the ability to create a folder that will automatically import files into notes—all you have to do is add a file to that folder, and it'll show up in Evernote in whichever notebook you specify as a new note. Here's how to get it set up:

1. Create a new folder somewhere on your computer, and call it something like "Add to Evernote."
2. In the Evernote application, select "Import Folders..." from the Tools menu. Click "Add" in the resulting window and select your "Add to Evernote" folder you just created and click "OK."

3. The folder will then appear in the Import folders list along with a few options.
4. If you want Evernote to also import items within folders that live inside "Add to Evernote", change "Subfolders" to "Yes".
5. If you'd like to change the notebook to which your imported content will be added, click the name of the notebook and select a different notebook from the dropdown list.
6. By default, Evernote will keep items that it imports from import folders. If you'd like files to be deleted from "Add to Evernote" after they're imported into Evernote, click "Keep" and choose "Delete" from the dropdown list.

Now, all you have to do to create a new note with one of your files is to drag or copy the file into your folder. That's it! And you can set up your scanner so that it saves all of your new scans into this folder so they'll be automatically and immediately imported into Evernote.

Finding Information

Now that you've had some practice capturing all sorts of information, you're going to want to know how to retrieve it. Storing your entire life in Evernote doesn't do you any good if you can't find it! Remember that because everything in your synchronized notebooks is stored online, you can use these search tools from any computer that's connected to the Internet, as well as other devices connected to your account.

1. Simple search

The easiest way to find one of your notes is just to search for it. The search bar is in the top-right corner of the screen, and it works just like any other search bar that you've ever used. Just type in what you're looking for, press enter, and the results will come up on your screen. You might wonder why you'd need other search methods, but once you've created a couple dozen notebooks and gotten over 500 notes or so (and trust me, it doesn't take long), your searches will start to return a lot more results than you can easily look through. However, this always works well as a first-line strategy.

2. Tags

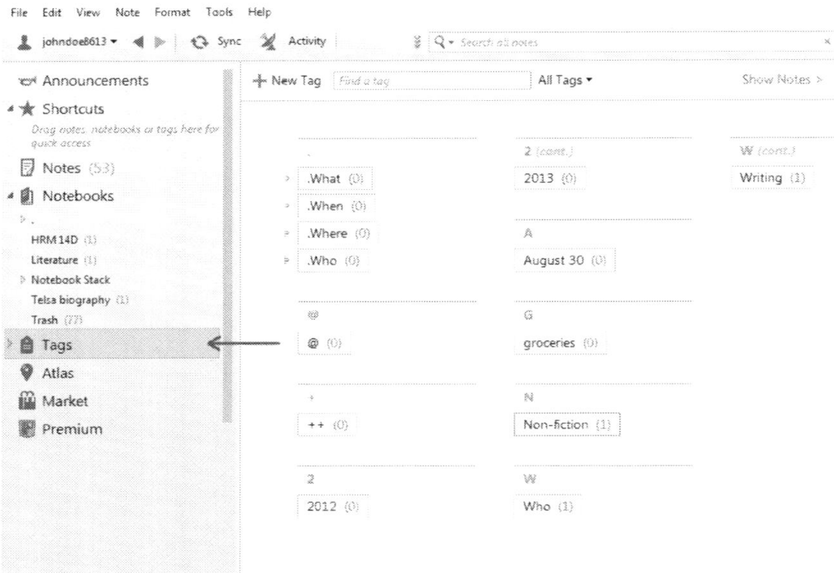

Remember when we talked about tagging your notes with useful words or phrases? This is where those come in handy. When you click on "Tags" in the sidebar, you'll see a list of all of your tags, and the number of notes that have those tags. Just double-click on one of the tags and you'll see all of the notes tagged with that term.

You can also run a simple search only within the notes that contain a certain tag, which allows you to pare down your results even further. Click on the search bar, type your search string, and click on the "Add Search Option" dropdown. There are a number of useful options here, including "Tag," "Source," and "Contains." I find the tag option here to be the most useful, but play around a bit and see which options you like the most.

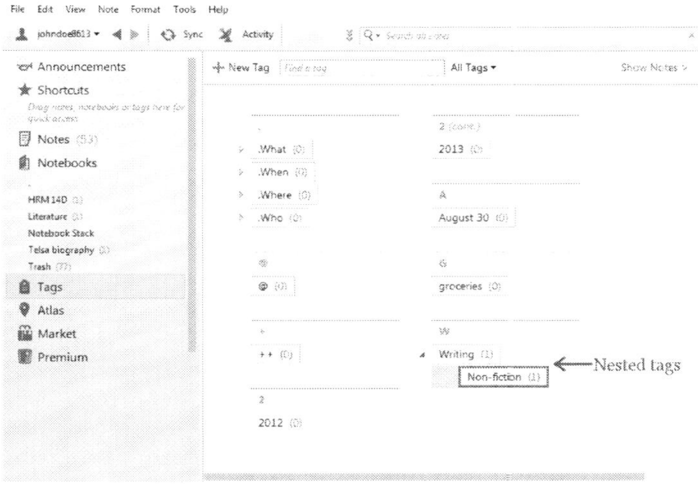

Evernote recently added the ability to create nested tags, which can be a huge help when looking through your tags if you've created a lot of them. In the Tags pane, just drag one tag on top of another one, and you'll have a nested tag. You can do this with a number of tags to make whatever sort of system you'd like. (To give you an example, I use a "courses" tag to hold all of the tags for the classes and workshops that I take; I don't tag anything with "courses," but it serves to hold them all in the same place.)

3. Title search

By adding the keyword "entitled" and a colon before your search term, you can search only note titles for that word or phrase. For example, you could search for "intitle: inventions" to find only notes that have the word "inventions" in the title. Make sure not to put a space after "intitle:", or this won't work.

4. Exclusive search

If you want to find some notes that *don't* include anything, you can add a dash before the search phrase. For example, you could search for "Tesla -Edison" to get notes that contain the word "Tesla" but don't contain "Edison." Again, this becomes useful once you start accumulating a lot of notes.

5. Exact search

Just like with most search engines, you can put quotes around your search phrase to return results that match that exact phrase only. If you search for "Tesla and The Prestige", you'll only get notes that contain that exact phrase.

6. Saved searches

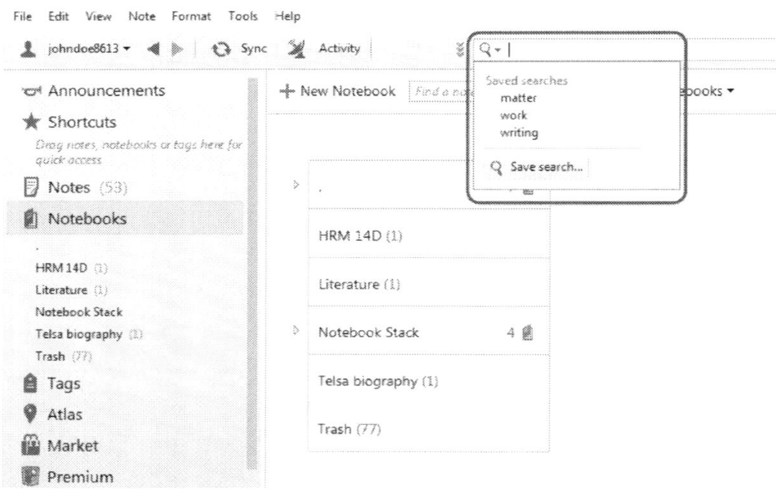

Many times, you'll find that you run the same search on a regular basis. For example, you might search for "content management" to see all of the notes that you've clipped for content management systems and tips on improving your web content. If you're a Windows user, just click "Save Search" below the search bar. On a Mac, run the search that you'd like to save, then click Edit > Find > Save Search. Now, whenever you click on the search bar, you'll see a section below your recent searches that contains all of your saved searches. If you want to edit one of those searches (to change the name of the search, change the search terms, or add search options), just click "Edit" next to the term on a Mac, or right-click the saved search and click on "Properties" on Windows.

One thing that was added in recent versions of Evernote that can save you even more time on saved searches is the ability to add your saved searches to the shortcuts section of the sidebar. Just click and drag the saved search from the saved searches list to the bar, and you'll be able to run your search with a single click. Think of a couple searches you're likely to run on a regular basis, and try saving one or two of them so you get the hang of it.

Managing Your Notes

Once you start using Evernote to store things that are useful for you, you're going to want to make sure that you can use your repository as efficiently as possible. Getting good at capturing and searching for information is a big part of this, but managing the notes that you've already created is also a good habit to get into. This section describes a few skills and habits that will help.

1. Regularly go through your notes.

Every once in a while, skim through two or three notebooks—quickly look through note titles and see if there's anything that you can delete or re-categorize. I find that after a few weeks, I have notes that I don't need anymore—vacation plans, to-do lists, idea lists, and things like that don't need to be stored forever. So just delete them! It'll free up space and make it easier to find more important things.

While you don't have to have a regular schedule for this, developing one isn't a bad idea. Put an event on your calendar on the first of every month to spend an hour going through your notes. This might seem a bit excessive—especially if your calendar is already packed—but it's absolutely worth it, especially if you're using a system like GTD. If Evernote is your organizational hub, it makes sense to spend a bit of extra time making sure that it's performing at its best!

2. Merge notes.

Once you've created a large number of notes, certain notebooks, stacks, and tags might start to get a bit overfilled. Fortunately, Evernote has a simple solution for this problem: you can merge a number of notes into a single note to save space. Just select all of the notes you want to merge (with a Ctrl + click or command + click), right-click on one of the notes, and select "Merge Notes." You can also use Note > Merge Notes from the menu bar. Remember that you can't unmerge notes—once you've turned them into a single note, there's no going back to individual ones without creating new notes and cutting / pasting the old content into the new ones.

3. Use notes to collaborate.

As a Premium user of Evernote, you can enable collaborative editing of specific notebooks and notes, which means that you can allow anyone else to make changes to those notes. If you're using Evernote in a professional context, this can be an invaluable tool.

To share a notebook, open the Notebooks tab from the sidebar and find the notebook that you want to share. Right-click on it and select "Share Notebook." Now, you have to decide whether you want to share it with a select group of people or make it open to the public. If you want others to be able to edit your notebook, you need to select "Share with individuals." Add the e-mail addresses of all the people you'd like to give access to the notebook, and select their level of access. There are four options:

1. view notes
2. view notes and activity
3. modify notes
4. modify notes and invite others

All you need to do is choose the option you want. If you're collaborating with co-workers, friends, or family, you'll probably want the third option, "modify notes." Now just add a message, and you're done! Once people have accepted your invitation, they'll be able to view and edit that notebook.

4. Create note templates.

If you use a specific kind of note on a regular basis, it might pay off to create a template. A great example of this is an order form. These forms always use the same fields, and it can be a pain to type in the date, customer name, customer number, order, price, delivery, and other field names. So instead, you can create a template that you can simply open and fill in. If you're using GTD, you can take advantage of note templates as well by creating a standard form for to-do or prioritization lists. There are two easy ways to do this, and I'll go through both of them here.

1. Use the export / import function.

The best part about this method is that it's relatively easy and doesn't require anything other than Evernote (while the next method requires another app). It does, however, take up a bit of space on your hard drive, and requires that you remember where you saved your templates. Here's how you go about it:

1. Use Evernote to create the template in a new note; add the fields that you'll need and anything else that will be included in every instance of that type of note.
2. Click on File > Export Note… and save the note with an informative name in a location that you'll remember.
3. To create a new note using that template, just open the notebook that you'd like to place it in and drag the note from Windows Explorer or Finder into that notebook.

That's all there is to it! To effectively use this strategy, I recommend creating a folder somewhere on your computer that contains all of your templates—that way you won't have to look around for them when you need to use one.

2. Use KustomNote.

KustomNote is a web and mobile app that lets you download templates that others have made, and it allows you to create your own for use with Evernote, Google Contacts, Google Calendar, and other apps like MailChimp. The public templates fall into categories like Workout, Conference, Customer, Focus Group, and a whole list of other useful groupings. Once you create a KustomNote account, you simply connect the app to your Evernote account and follow the instructions for creating new templates. You can then create notes online that will be saved to your Evernote account and be easily accessible from your desktop client.

While you can use KustomNote for free, you can opt for a premium account that costs either $1.99 or $3.99 per month, both of which can get you some upgraded features, like the ability to create offline notes, removing ads, and private team template sharing. Whether or not you need these features is up to you, but both options are pretty inexpensive, so it's worth thinking about.

To find out more about KustomNote or to sign up for an account, go to www.kustomnote.com.

Using Evernote at Home and at Work

Now that you have a pretty good idea of how to use Evernote, I'm going to give you a bunch of different ideas on how to make use if it in your life. Some of these tips are my own, and some come from others, but they're all backed up with experience. You can use these just like they're described, modify them for your own use, or use them as inspiration to make up your own uses for Evernote. No matter what you do, have fun with it, and don't be afraid to experiment!

Using Evernote for Your Finances

Much of this list comes from a blog post on *The Simple Dollar* by Trent Hamm, an author and blogger who uses Evernote. If you're looking for more good information on household finances, check Trent out—he has a lot of good things to say!

1. Record spending on the go.

Remember when everyone wrote down all of their purchases in a checkbook? With debit cards, contactless payments, and other modern financial technologies, this has fallen by the wayside, and it's become a bit more difficult to keep track of what you're spending. But Evernote can help! Just create a notebook called "Spending" and keep track of everything you spend while you're out. Making a new note with few words to describe your purchase and the total price takes just a moment, and you'll have a much better handle on where your money's going.

2. Track prices for comparison shopping.

Comparison shopping is a great way to save money, but it's often overlooked. And without a central place for storing this information, you might forget what you should be buying at which stores. But with a few notes dedicated to comparison shopping, you'll always know where to find the best prices!

3. Take notes on potential investments.

Getting ideas for good investments may come unexpectedly—maybe a good piece of news will come to you while you're at the pub, or maybe you'll come across something interesting on your phone while riding the bus. A quick jot on a note will help you remember to do further research when you get home and have the time.

4. Keep track of gift ideas.

Combining this with the tip above on comparison shopping can help make gift shopping a lot easier. I know that I've struggled with this before—when you wait until the last minute because you don't have a good idea, you tend not to make the best choices. But if you're keeping a list of great gift ideas alongside the best places to buy those gifts, you'll be a step ahead when Christmas or birthdays are just around the corner.

5. Keep a list of automated transactions.

With all of the things that you pay for automatically (some of your utility bills, your Netflix and Spotify subscriptions, charitable donations, and any number of other things), it can be easy to forget where your money is going. But if you keep a list of the amounts and dates of automated transactions, you'll be better informed about your expenditures, and you'll also be able to look at your list to see if you should hold off on spending money until after a certain transaction has cleared.

Using Evernote at Home

No matter what you're trying to do at home, Evernote can help you stay organized and on task. I use Evernote for all kinds of things at home, and this is just an introduction to a few of them.

1. Planning and documenting home improvement.

Whether you're renovating a room or re-organizing your closet, proper planning will help you. Going to install some new shelves to keep your garage organized? Use the web clipper to store some ideas from home improvement blogs. Re-tiling your floor? Keep a list of your favorite tiles and how much they cost. Hiring a contractor? Create a note with names, phone numbers, and estimates.

And once you get started, why not document the process? Use Evernote to organize photos, journal entries, videos, and anything else you want to remember about your home improvement project. If you're keeping all of these things in disparate places, this can be a monumental task. But with Evernote, it's as easy as creating a few notes and attaching some files.

2. Track organization ideas.

This is something I do on a regular basis—I like to keep everything in my home well-organized, so I keep a notebook of potential organization strategies and products to help in this endeavor. I have notes that detail ways to keep cupboards and closets organized, notes with cool storage ideas, and notes with things I'd like to buy to keep my things organized. If I ever want to improve the organization of a room or part of a room, all I have to do is open up that notebook, and I have a bunch of good ideas. And because I clip these whenever I come across them, I don't have to go searching the Internet whenever I need some inspiration.

3. Plan a redecoration.

When you're redecorating, you might have an idea in your head that's hard to articulate. But with Evernote, you can keep photos of color swatches, magazine articles with cool ideas, and pictures of rooms that you like all in one place. And by keeping them all together, you can generate a good idea of what your room (or entire home) will look like once you're done.

You can take this a step further by creating multiple notes with potential redecoration plans. For example, keep one note with some of your favorite ideas for blue rooms, and another with ideas for yellow rooms. Or if you can't decide whether your basement should be a home entertainment center or an office, keep a few notes about the benefits and drawbacks of both, as well as some plans and photos that you like.

4. Keep an inventory.

A home inventory can be a very useful thing—when you're moving in with someone, when you're submitting an insurance claim, or when you're planning a move. Doing a home inventory all at once can be a daunting task, but if you start it early and do a room or two at a time, it can be a whole lot easier. And by keeping each room's list separate from the others, they become much more manageable.

Because it's so easy to add photos to your notes, you can take pictures of your possessions to add to the inventory. This is especially useful for collections or if someone else might need to reference your inventory.

5. Organize your recipes.

Recipe books, files, and folders can be a huge mess—you get index cards from some people, you print out other recipes, you write down a recipe you see on the news, and you clip others from the newspaper. Pretty soon, you'll have a big pile of recipes scribbled on scraps of paper in your hands with no good way to store them. But by scanning or typing them into Evernote, you can keep them all in a single, central location.

And with notebooks and tags, you can keep them even more organized—my personal recipe notebooks include Breakfast, Lunch, Dinner, Soups / Chilis, and Sides. And I have tags like "Indian," "Mexican," "oatmeal," "vegetarian" and "dairy-free." This makes it really easy when I want to find a recipe that meets a very specific set of criteria!

Using Evernote at Work

Although Evernote can be a lifesaver in any area of your life, I find it to be most useful when it comes to my professional life. As an author, I use it all the time—and when I'm collaborating on projects with others, it's a lifesaver. There are dozens and dozens of ways Evernote can help you at work, but these nine tips are my favorite.

1. Share and collaborate.

No matter where you work, you're almost sure to work with a team. By sharing notes, you can make sure that everyone in your team has access to the information that they need. And they don't even need to use Evernote to see it! All they need is a web browser and an Internet connection to see the notes you've shared.

If they do use Evernote, you have even more power to collaborate—you can make your notebooks and notes editable, so that anyone can add or edit content, which is fantastic when you need a central repository for things that are used for your team, or if you just want to keep a running log of what everyone's doing. One of the greatest benefits of using Evernote for such purposes is that it will reduce the amount of e-mails exchanged within the team, which everyone will appreciate.

2. Organize research.

This is especially important for people in professions like mine, but almost everyone needs to do a little research at some point or another. Whether you're looking up articles on Wikipedia, calling other companies, asking questions around the organization, or reading scholarly articles, it's helpful to keep everything that you've learned in a central location that's easily accessible and searchable. With Evernote, you can read and search your notes from anywhere where there's an Internet connection. And if you have a Premium account, you can download your notebooks to your mobile devices for offline access, meaning you can even read them when you're, say, on a plane trip.

How you use Evernote for research organization is up to you—notebooks, notes, tags… you can use all of these to segregate information by subject, date, project, or any other sort of characteristic that you find useful. I tend to create stacks for different areas of work (clients, personal development, career planning) and notebooks for smaller divisions (individual clients, personal projects, development courses, and so on).

3. Prepare for and document meetings.

Just about everyone appreciates the need for more effective, more efficient meetings. If you're one of the people who spend a good portion of their day in meetings, you should see the utility of Evernote for this purpose immediately. You can use it to prepare your own materials—presentation notes, questions for others, recaps of previous events—or you can use the collaborative features to help everyone come to the meeting well-prepared. For example, let everyone record the questions they'd like answered in a single document where everyone else can see them so people come prepared to discuss what they need to. Or add documents to a shared note so that your colleagues can review them (and post revisions, if they'd like) before the meeting.

After the meeting, you can easily share notes, tasks, and questions with other team members. You can even do this before you get out of the meeting room! This will help you accomplish what needs to get done faster and prepare everyone for the next meeting.

4. Plan your weeks and use time wisely.

Although Evernote isn't built as a task list app, it works really well as one. By adding a checkbox before all of the things you need to do (just click the checkbox icon in the toolbar in the note editor), you can check off what you've gotten done and see at a glance what you need to accomplish throughout the rest of the week. If you're using GTD, this will be built right into your use of Evernote, and everything will be assigned a priority level so you never have to wonder what you should be doing at any given time.

You can take this a step further by creating notes and notebooks centered on certain tasks—this is especially useful with repeating tasks, like a weekly sales report or team update. Create a note for this week, record everything you need, and then reference it in your preparation. Then, if you need to remember what happened last week, it'll be right in your note list already. No need to e-mail around asking or wrack your brain trying to remember.

5. Create a customized customer relations management (CRM) system.

Organizations spend thousands of dollars (and, I would imagine, much more) on highly complex software systems from creators like Oracle and Sales Force when many of them could just be using a free system like Evernote! You could use stacks to categorize potential clients and current customers into groups—potential, current, past; local, online; or even break them down by division—and then use notebooks to further break them down. Each note could contain contact information for the customer, order history, interests, notes, and anything else you could possibly need.

This will work best for small- to medium-sized businesses, but it's not hard to imagine this method working well for a large organization as well. By leveraging stacks, notebooks, notes, tags, and search functions, you should have no problem keeping track of all of your clients. And with reminders (which I'll discuss shortly), you can even get an e-mail reminding you to get in touch with a client on a certain day.

6. Brainstorm.

Whether you have brainstorming sessions in a large group or you do it by yourself, keeping all of your ideas and potential projects in one place is very valuable—especially if everyone in your team can see them. Store all of your ideas in a single place, and make sure everyone browses through them on occasion to see if they trigger new ideas, or if any of your old concepts now seem better-fitted to your current needs. There's no reason to throw away any of your old ideas—just keep them in an archive somewhere for future inspiration. Reviewing these ideas doesn't take long, and it could pay off in a big way if you're inspired to make effective changes for your company, or you come up with a great product idea.

7. Preparing for tax season.

This is a good idea for both companies and individuals, but because it's generally more complicated for businesses, I've included it here. One of the things that makes preparing taxes such a pain is that you need so many different documents. But if you have them all scanned into Evernote, it's a breeze! You'll have your tax forms, your contractors' tax forms, and any other sort of information that you'll need right at your fingertips. You can keep them all in a single notebook for referencing on your return forms or your tax software; or, if you have someone else prepare your taxes, you can just send it all right over.

By keeping this kind of information in Evernote throughout the year, you can make doing your taxes relatively painless—you won't have to go digging for receipts of charitable donations your company made (just search for the tag "charitable") or your latest income reports (just look in the Income Reports notebook). While starting to use Evernote right at the last minute will be helpful, starting earlier is even better.

8. Organize travel documents.

If more than one person is travelling in your company, it can be a hassle to keep everything organized—receipts, tickets, itineraries, and so on can get lost in e-mail accounts, filing systems, and paper inboxes. But by adding all of those things to Evernote, you can not only keep your own travel documents organized, but you can help everyone in the company stay on top of travel plans by using a public notebook. That way everyone can look in the central repository when they need to find out about their own travel plans or others'.

9. Manage ordering and fulfillment.

If you really want to keep everything in the same place, you can use Evernote for ordering and fulfillment as well—whether you use a standard order form for your customers or if they do it by e-mail, all you have to do is copy and paste (or drag and drop) the order record into a new note, and you now have a record of it that anyone can access. And by creating different notebooks for pending orders, fulfilled orders, and any other categories you might need, your entire ordering record can be kept in Evernote! This is another tip that is more likely to work better for small- or medium-sized businesses, but if you're diligent about checking and updating the app, you could probably use it even for a decently large national business.

If you're going to be using Evernote to manage your business, you might want to look into Evernote Business, which gives you added sharing and management capabilities for a large group of people. You can easily create shared and personal notebooks; billing is simplified for large groups; and you get business-level administration and support. If you're working by yourself or with just a couple of others, a Premium account or two might be more efficient, but if you're interested in getting your whole company up and running with Evernote, I recommend checking out www.evernote.com/business to get the details on all of the added benefits of business-level subscription.

Using Evernote for Fun

So far, I've been discussing Evernote for business settings; managing your personal life and daily tasks; managing your finances; and collaborating with your team; but Evernote isn't all about being more productive. You can also use it for a lot of fun things, too! As I've mentioned a few times, you're only limited by what you can imagine—so read over these tips and think about how you might be able to use Evernote to help you have more fun in your life.

1. Plan a party.

Whether you're going to be hosting a dinner party or you're responsible for organizing a family (or school) reunion, it can be helpful to have one central place to keep all of the related information. Keep invitation lists, invitation responses, ideas for food and games, notes, gifts, and anything else you could possibly need to make your party a success. Share photos and videos after the event, write thank-you notes, and start planning the next party all from a single app.

2. Motivate yourself to do something new.

Taking on a challenging new goal can be awfully intimidating—losing weight, getting in shape, learning a new language, reading a challenging book, or learning a new skill can seem like a monumental task when you're just getting started. But Evernote can help you stay motivated, monitor your progress, and organize your useful materials so that you'll be able to stay on track to achieve your goals.

Keep a schedule of tasks or goals, and make notes when you meet (or miss) them. Clip useful articles that you find on the Internet about meeting your goals or staying motivated through tough times. Track your progress—write down how many calories you ate in a day, how many minutes you ran, how much weight you lifted, how long you practiced French, or how many pages you read. Keep a note with rewards so you know that you're getting closer and that you will feel eager to reach a big milestone. Whatever you're doing, Evernote can help you plan, prepare for, and meet your goals.

3. Make a scrapbook.

Scrapbooking is a popular pastime, but not everyone wants to buy scrapbooks and all of the materials required to fill them. Using Evernote (along with a photo-annotation tool like Skitch) will allow you to build a scrapbook right on your computer, complete with pictures, fun text, and notes. You can clip Facebook posts, tweets, videos, audio clips, and all sorts of things into these scrapbooks that can't be printed or pasted on a paper book. And getting photos into Evernote is a whole lot faster than cutting and gluing photos onto paper, so it's a hobby you can try without a significant investment of time.

4. Keep a memory file for your kids.

If you were to keep everything that your kids brought home from school—paintings, drawings, projects, good grades—you'd have a huge heap of files within a couple of years. But if you scan or photograph them and put them in Evernote, you'll be able to keep them forever without taking up an entire closet. Take videos of your child's play performances, photos of their science fair projects, scans of their papers, and records of their grades. Then, when you want to look back, you'll know exactly where to go—no more digging around in a closet or the garage trying to find memories for your high schooler's graduation party—they're all in one place!

5. Make a vacation diary.

This is a combination of some of the above ideas—take photos and videos of your vacation, and write little notes about what you did while you were there. What was your favorite item at the British Museum? Which Hawaiian island did you like the most? What's the story behind your favorite picture from the trip? Did you run into someone you knew? Did you find out some really interesting facts? All of these things can be quickly jotted into Evernote and later organized into a very fun vacation report that you can easily share online.

6. Manage a collection.

Do you collect something? Baseball cards? Vintage cars? Thimbles? Shot glasses? China? Model airplanes? All of these things can be photographed and documented with Evernote—snap a picture, enter any useful details about the object, and write down anything interesting that you might want to remember. Then, if you want to show off your collection, you have a big stack of pictures and interesting information that you can share! And if you're trying to remember something about a specific item in your collection, you can just reference that notebook in Evernote instead of looking through your collection and wracking your brain trying to remember where you picked up this particular item.

7. Make a wish list.

If you have any sort of wishlist—vacations you'd like to take, restaurants you'd like to visit, cars you'd like to own, races you'd like to run—Evernote provides a great way to organize and track that list. For example, I have a list of attractions and restaurants that I'd like to visit in London. Whenever I go to one of them, I put a checkmark next to the name and jot down a quick note about how that place was. "Great pizza," "cheap drinks," "too expensive," "long wait," and other things like that help me remember the places that I want to go back to and those I want to avoid forever.

Using Evernote at School

In my postgraduate years, I had a great need for organization. With courses, workshops, teaching, and research, I had a huge amount of information that was competing for attention and—before I started using Evernote—getting lost. Once I realized how much Evernote could help, I started using it almost constantly, and I became well-organized almost overnight. I've recommended Evernote to a lot of students, and most of them have thanked me for it. Most of these tips are for university-level students, but they can easily be applied to high school students, and possibly even middle school as well.

1. Organize your class notes.

Whether you're in high school or working toward your PhD, you're probably taking a lot of classes, and you're also probably taking notes in those classes. One of the best ways you can use Evernote is to create a stack for class notes, and a new notebook for each class. Add a new note to the notebook for each class day (or book chapter) and take your notes there. Now, whenever you need to review for a test or get ideas for a paper, you'll have everything that you've talked about in that class in a single place that you can easily reference. You can also add electronic versions of the syllabus, lecture slides, and anything else that might be useful for that class.

2. Plan a paper.

When you're writing a paper, it's best to get your ideas down before you start writing—do some brainstorming, write an outline, or just throw down a bunch of keywords into a file and go from there. Whatever your preferred strategy, Evernote can help by keeping everything you need—plans, resources, drafts—organized and easily accessible. And because you can easily edit files on your phone or tablet, you can jot down any good ideas that you have while on the run so you don't forget by the time you get back to your desk.

One of the things that I find to be really useful is to keep quotations from books and articles in a notebook so I can use them in my next paper or assignment. I write down the quote, the author, the book or article, and the page. I do this as I'm reading so I don't have to try to remember where I read something two weeks ago when I'm already stressed about getting my paper done on time!

3. Create your own study guide.

Studying for a test is most effective when your study materials are well-organized. It should be obvious by now how Evernote could help you out here—copy and paste relevant notes from other notebooks into a new one for studying. Write practice answers to questions you might see on the test. Take notes on what your professor tells you might be on the exam. Make a study schedule to keep yourself on track so you make sure to cover everything before the day of the test.

One really useful tool that you can use for this purpose is Evernote Peek, a separate app for the iPad that allows you to easily turn your notes into flashcards—to use them, just lift up the smart cover a bit to expose the question, then lift it more to expose the answer. If you got it right, mark the question correct and move onto the next one. If you got it wrong, mark it incorrect, and it'll show up again until you get it right. This is a hugely useful tool that can be used for all sorts of things.

4. Keep career-planning resources.

When you're getting ready to graduate from high school or college, you'll likely start to wonder about what you might want to do with your life, and this can be a really stressful endeavor. Keep notes on careers you're interested in, salary comparisons, educational requirements, information sessions, and other career-related items in a notebook so that you can look at them all in the same place instead of searching for all of the information on Google again.

Advanced Tips and Tricks

I hope you appreciate now just how useful Evernote can be in almost every area of your life. With the information that you've read so far in this book, you're all set to start using Evernote to keep your life organized, efficient, and productive. But Evernote has even more tricks up its sleeve—and in this section, you'll be learning some of the advanced techniques you can use to take advantage of Evernote's full potential.

Get Note Reminders

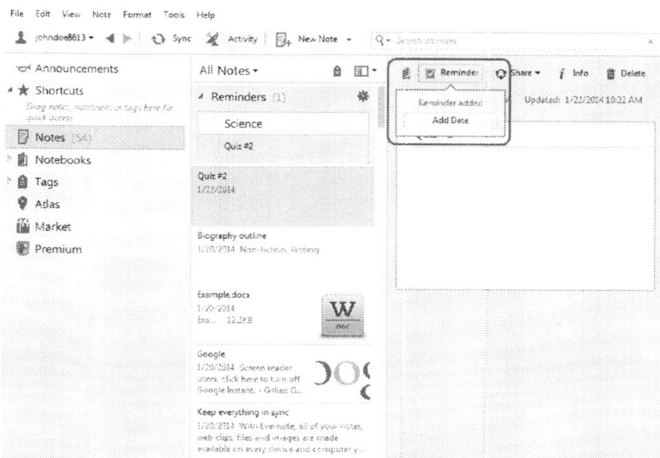

If you have a note that needs your attention on a certain date, you can set up a reminder so Evernote will e-mail and alert you on the day so you can do whatever you need to do. This is especially great if you're using Evernote for GTD, as you'll want to archive notes to deal with later. Even if you're not using Evernote for this purpose, it's good to know how to create reminders—I find that I use them all the time for a wide variety of things. It's a quite simple process.

1. Open the note you'd like to add a reminder to.
2. Click the icon that looks like a clock with a check mark in it.
3. Click "Add a Date" to choose when to receive your reminder.

That's it! Now you'll be reminded when your note is due. Of course, it's still up to you to accomplish whatever needs to be done, but this will help keep you from losing notes after you save them. You can always click the clock again and hit "Mark as Done" or "Clear Reminder" to cancel the reminder.

Use IFTTT to Automate Your Note-taking Process

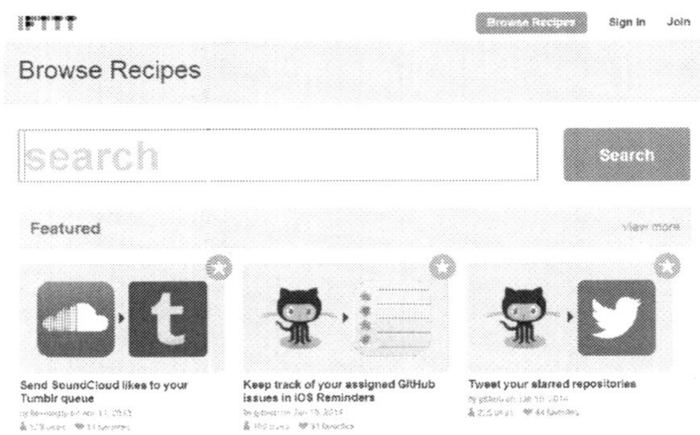

If This, Then That (IFTTT) is an online app that can make your life a lot easier. The concept behind IFTTT is very simple—when one thing happens, another thing happens. You set up trigger events and response events, and whenever one of the triggers takes place, the response happens. For example, you can set up a recipe (the trigger / response pairs are called recipes) that will download all your tweets into a Google spreadsheet. You could also create one that will e-mail you every photo you take on your iPhone.

There are tons of different ways you can use IFTTT with Evernote; some of the most popular options include sending starred e-mails from Gmail to Evernote, sending Instagram photos to Evernote, adding new contacts to Evernote, and creating a Google Calendar event from an Evernote note. IFTTT allows you to create recipes with a huge number of applications and websites, so the possibilities are almost limitless! Evernote, Gmail, LinkedIn, Facebook, Twitter, Pocket, Wordpress, Feedly, Flickr, Craigslist, ESPN, The *New York Times*, YouTube, and a lot of actions taken from your phone can all be involved in your IFTTT recipes.

To find out more about how it works and see the full list of sites and apps that work with the service, visit www.ifttt.com.

Use Evernote to Post to Facebook, Twitter, and Linkedin

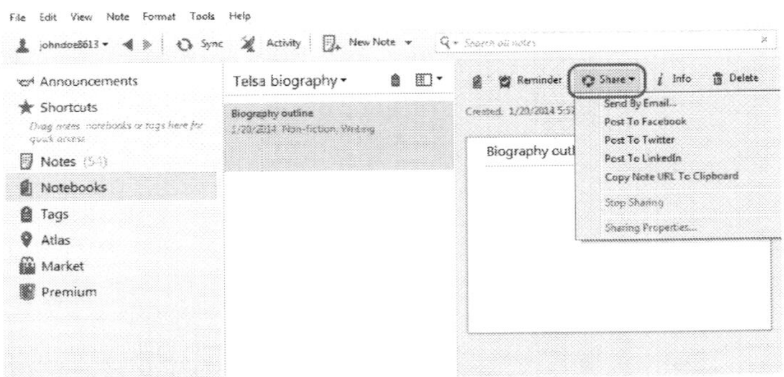

Evernote has built-in support for posting your notes to these three social networks, which can be really useful when you want to share your information with the world (or just a few people; whichever fits your particular situation). To share a note, just click on the Share button at the top of a note in the note editor and select the network that you want to share on. A new window will open in your browser, and you'll need to sign into that network (unless you're already signed in, in which case you can just hit "post"). Once you've done that, share away!

When you publicly share a note like this, Evernote creates a public link to your note online, which means that anyone who has the link will be able to see your note. Because of this, it's not advisable to share any sort of private or confidential information this way, just in case somebody accidentally shares the link with a bunch of other people. If you'd like to share any sort of private information, it's best to simply share a notebook with only the people who need to see it.

E-mail Directly to Evernote

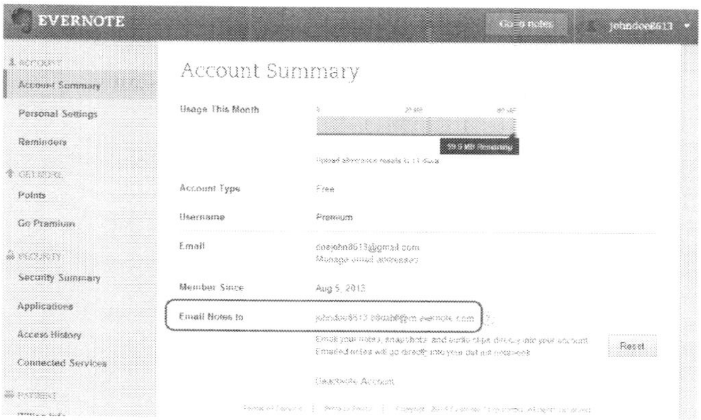

One thing that many people don't know about—but could actually really benefit from—is that you can e-mail things directly to your Evernote account. Just write up a note in your e-mail client, hit send, and it'll show up in your app! It's pretty cool, and can actually be really useful. To find the address that you need to send your notes to, log into your online Evernote account (on www.evernote.com), click on your name in the upper right-hand corner, and click "Account Settings." In your Account Summary, you'll see "Email notes to" and an e-mail address. Add that to your contact list under "Evernote" (or whatever you'd like), and all you have to do is start typing the word Evernote into your to: field and you're set! Now type away and send yourself a note. You can also forward e-mails from your inbox directly to your account, which is really great when you want to get all of the contents of the e-mail and any attachments directly into a notebook without copying and pasting.

To get even more use out of this trick, you can add tags to your notes by adding a hashtag (#) and an already-existing tag to the subject line of the e-mail. For example, if you get an e-mail about

Nikola Tesla, you could forward it to yourself and add the #inventions tag to the subject line (this only works with tags that you've already used in Evernote; you can't add new ones this way). You can also send your notes to specific notebooks by adding the "at" symbol (@) and the name of the notebook to the subject line. So by typing @writing in the subject, it'll go to your Writing notebook.

Keep Important Tags and Notebooks at the Top of Your Lists

All of your stacks, notebooks, and tags automatically get alphabetized, and are displayed in alphabetical order. Most of the time, this is fine, because alphabetization makes it easy to find things. However, if you use a specific tag or notebook a lot, you might want to make sure that it doesn't fall down the list. All you have to do is add a special character to the beginning of the notebook or tag name. For example, if you need to use your Research notebook more often than most of the others, rename it !Research, and it'll stay right at the top of the list.

You can use other characters too, including @ and # (in case you're wondering, ! Goes to the top of the list, @ comes next, and # is third). By using these symbols, you can get around the automatic alphabetization. Don't go too crazy with these, though—eventually, you might find that there are too many notebooks and tags that automatically go to the top of your list and you'll have to reorganize again!

Use Note Links to Reference Other Notes

Once you start using Evernote to classify and organize everything in your life, you'll probably start finding that some notes are difficult to put into a single category. For example, does research on the price of a new home go into Home or Finance? Fortunately, there's a pretty easy solution for this: note links. Note links are very similar to the hyperlinks that you use on the Internet, except that when you click on one, it'll bring to another note instead of a web page.

To create a link, open the note that you're going to add the link to. Then right-click on the note that you'd like to create the link to in the note list, and select "Copy Note Link." Now go back to the note that you want to create the link in and click Edit > Paste (or use a standard keyboard shortcut for paste) to add the link. Now, when you click the link, the other note will open in the note editor.

This might not seem like a big deal at first, but once you get up to a few hundred notes, this will become a really useful tool for keeping track of where you've placed certain information.

Interface with Other Apps, Sites, and Devices

This is the final tip of this section, and this is what will truly make you an Evernote master. I've already talked about a couple of scanners that work with Evernote, and I've given you an idea of what IFTTT can do for your workflow. But you can use a lot more tools than these to further increase your productivity and level of organization. I've included just a small sampling of some of best apps that you can use with Evernote here, but there are a lot more, and new ones are added all the time. To get a better idea of what you can use directly with Evernote, visit appcenter.evernote.com. There, you can see a huge list of Windows, Mac, iPhone, iPad, Android, and web apps.

Windows apps

Foxit Reader (www.foxitsoftware.com)

Foxit is a lightweight PDF reader that allows you to read, sign, and print PDF files. And it interfaces directly with Evernote, so you can import PDFs right into one of your notebooks. This is great for filing receipts, contracts, and any other sort of document that you often receive in PDF format. And with the Microsoft Word extension, you can instantly save any document to PDF.

Price: free (reader version), there are also many higher-level creation options, starting at $89.99.

Mac apps

PDFPen (www.smilesoftware.com)

PDFPen provides similar functionality to Foxit Reader, described above, but is available for OS X. Add text and images to your PDFs, scan hand-written or printed text, add signatures, and save directly to Evernote from the File menu. While this is an expensive app, it's worth looking into if you spend a lot of time working with PDFs.

Price: $59.95 (free trial available).

Windows / Mac

CallNote (www.kandasoft.com)

Skype is becoming increasingly popular as a way to communicate both at home and at work, and Kanda has created a very convenient little app for recording your Skype calls. CallNote records the audio from your calls (the free premium version can also record chats and screen sharing), and you can instantly save the recording as a note in Evernote, where you can listen to the conversation again, take notes, and share the recording. Although the 25 / 100MB file size limit might cause some difficulties for longer conversations, this is a great app for helping you remember what happened on a call.

Price: free (basic and premium versions), $19.95 / year (professional version).

Clarify (www.clarify-it.com)

When you need to explain to someone (or a group of people) how to do something, sending screenshots can be extremely helpful. But it can take a long time to get all of the screenshots you need with one app, annotate them with another, and use a third one to get them into the same document. Clarify makes this a simple process and includes a number of useful features, like a countdown timer and keyboard shortcuts. And once you've created your document, you can import it directly into Evernote, ready to be shared with the world (or at least your company).

Price: $29.99 (free 14-day trial).

iOS apps

CamScanner (www.camscanner.net)

CamScanner allows you to use the camera on your iPhone or iPad to capture documents or pictures and import them directly into Evernote. This is great for when you get receipts while you're on the road, when you want to have a colleague review a contract before you sign it, or when you just see something fun that you want to have a record of. The free version of CamScanner includes ads and watermarks, but it'll still give you a good scan of the document you want.

Price: free (basic version), $4.99 / month or $49.99 / year (premium version).

EverClip (www.clip.ignition.hk)

What the Web Clipper does for your desktop, EverClip does for your iPhone or iPad. You can use this app to clip things from your browser and other apps directly into notes in Evernote, removing the painful process of copying and pasting on a phone. You can also combine multiple clips into a single note, which is great when you're conducting a bit of light research on the bus.

Price: $2.99.

Android apps

HulloMail (www.hullomail.com)

This is a really cool app that allows you to read text versions of your voicemails, and with Evernote integration, you can import those voicemails directly into one of your notebooks. This is very useful when you don't have time to listen to all of your voicemails (especially if you're someone who gets a lot of them), but you want to have access to them at all times. You can read a few of them between meetings or skim them all when you get home.

Price: free (basic version).

StringNote (www.kandasoft.com)

As fast as Evernote is, sometimes you just don't have time to create a new note and type in a title and some notes. StringNote solves this problem by allowing you to double-click your power button to quickly create a picture, video, or audio note that will be saved to Evernote with your current location and time in the title field, so you can go back and edit the note later. With StringNote, it's next to impossible to forget things!

Price: free.

As I mentioned, this is just a small number of the apps that you can use to enhance your Evernote experience. There are even other Evernote apps (Evernote Hello, Evernote Clearly, Evernote Food, Evernote Peek, Penultimate, Skitch) that are made expressly to improve your productivity through Evernote. I highly recommend checking them out and seeing how you can use them to improve your workflow.

About the Author

Dominic Wolff is an author, business owner and traveller (or as he likes to call it, a globe trotter). A native from Idaho, Dominic became interested in the mechanics of business from a very young age. From those early days of selling candy bars to running a multi-state company today, Dominic has always been on the lookout for systems that would improve his productivity and allow him more free time to enjoy his hobbies. He frequently writes articles about personal productivity for business publications.

He believes that having a structure in place for work and life can mean the difference between being in control and merely coping.

An avid collector of fine red wines, he also owns a small wine boutique stocking only the finest of Washington, Oregon and Idaho wines. During his travels to far and wonderful places he also searches for the absolute best Zinfandel that can rival those of California. He lives in Wyoming with his wife Sarah, two German Shepherds and a tiny vineyard of his own.

Conclusion

By now, you should be feeling very comfortable with Evernote. You can create notes, notebooks, and stacks, and do a number of different things with them. You can create nested tags and use them to keep your notebooks well-organized. You can create reminders, share and collaborate with others, post notes on social networking sites, e-mail notes to yourself, and link between notes. You have all the skills of an Evernote master, and you're ready to get started organizing your life!

The last piece of advice that I'll give you is one that I've mentioned a few times throughout the book: don't be afraid to experiment with new kinds of organization. I've given you some ideas on how to sort your information, but your life is different from mine—if you think something might work better for you, try it! Trying out different things is best done early on in your Evernote career, because re-tagging, re-sorting, and re-naming takes more time when you have a huge number of notes and notebooks. It's certainly not impossible (I have almost 1,000 notes and I still do it from time to time), but it's a bit easier in the beginning. So play around with it and see what's best for you.

Now, go forth, document, categorize, and organize! Use Evernote to improve your life, and spread the word. We could all use better organization tools. And don't forget to support Evernote as a company—with the recent demise of Google Reader, a beloved free service, it's become clear that if we don't monetarily support the services that we use, we run the risk of losing them. So if you use Evernote a lot, upgrade to the Premium version!

One Last Thing...

Thank you so much for reading my book. I hope you really liked it. As you probably know, many people look at the reviews before they decide to purchase a book. If you liked the book, could you please take a minute to leave a review with your feedback? 60 seconds is all I'm asking for, and it would mean the world to me.

Dominic Wolff

Images and Cover by Organized Living Press

ORGANIZED LIVING
PRESS

Atlanta, Georgia USA

8461794R00049

Printed in Great Britain
by Amazon.co.uk, Ltd.,
Marston Gate.